HOW OUR BODIES WORK

BIRTH AND GROWTH

JAN BURGESS

Editorial planning
Philip Steele

SILVER BURDETT PRESS

Copyright © 1988 by Schoolhouse Press, Inc.
an imprint of Silver Burdett Inc.
Prentice Hall Building, Route 9W,
Englewood Cliffs, N.J. 07632

Original copyright, © Macmillan Education Limited 1988
© BLA Publishing Limited 1988

Designed and produced by BLA Publishing Limited,
East Grinstead, Sussex, England.

A Ling Kee Company

Illustrations by David Anstey; Sallie Alane Reason; Val
Sangster/Linden Artists and Linda Thursby/Linden Artists
Printed in Hong Kong

88/89/90/91/92/93   6 5 4 3 2 1

Library of Congress Cataloging-in-Publication Data

Burgess, Janet, 1952–
  Birth and growth
  (How our bodies work)
  Includes index.
  Summary: Explains how babies are born, grow, become
children, then adults, and eventually die.
  1. Human growth — Juvenile literature. 2. Childbrith —
Juvenile literature. 3. Developmental biology — Juvenile
literature. [1. Growth]
I. Title. II. Series.

QP84.R86   1988   612'.6   88-1925

ISBN 0-382-09708-4

Photographic credits

t = top b = bottom l = left r = right

cover: Trevor Hill

4 S. & R. Greenhill; 5t, 5b Frank Lane Picture Agency;
6 ZEFA; 11, 13 Science Photo Library; 15t Trevor Hill;
15b, 16 S. & R. Greenhill; 17 Rex Features; 18 Camilla
Jessel; 19 Science Photo Library; 20 ZEFA; 21, 22t, 22b,
23, 24, 25t Trevor Hill; 25b, 26, 27t Camilla Jessel;
27b, 28, 29t Trevor Hill; 29b S. & R. Greenhill; 30, 31,
32, 33t Trevor Hill; 33b, 34t, 34b S. & R. Greenhill;
35 Camilla Jessel; 36 Rex Features; 37t The Hutchison
Library; 37b Rex Features; 38, 39t Trevor Hill; 39b, 40t
S. & R. Greenhill; 40b Rex Features; 41 Trevor Hill; 42,
43t, 43b The Hutchison Library

How To Use This Book:

This book has many useful features. For example, look at the table of contents. See how it describes
each section in the book. Find a section you want to read and turn to it.

Notice that the section is a "two-page spread." That is, it covers two facing pages. Now look at
the headings in the spread. Headings are useful when you want to locate specific information. Next,
look at a photograph, drawing, chart or map and find its caption. Captions give you additional
information. A chart or map may also have labels to help you.

Scan the spread for a word in **bold print**. If you cannot find one in this spread, find one in
another spread. Bold-print words are defined in the glossary at the end of the book. Find your
bold-print word in the glossary.

Now turn to the index at the end of the book. When you have a specific topic or subject to
research, look for it in the index. you will quickly know whether the topic is in the book.

We hope you will use the features in this book to help you learn about new and exciting things.

Contents

Introduction

The story of how a baby is born and how it grows up is one of the most amazing that there is. Many animals take only a few weeks or months to become adults. Human babies take much longer.

It is about twenty years from the time a human baby is born until it becomes an adult and stops growing. All this time, the young human is learning new things about the world around him or her.

Animals and Eggs

All animals, including humans, eventually get old and die. New young animals grow up to take their places. This is vital if each kind of animal, or **species**, is to survive. The way creatures make new copies of themselves is known as **reproduction**.

Some species reproduce differently from others. Simple animals, such as an amoeba, just divide in half. An amoeba has no fixed shape and lives in water. When it divides, each half swims away, a complete amoeba. The problem with this kind of reproduction is that it does not allow for any change in the animal. The children are exactly the same as the parent, that is, they are **identical**.

More complex animals have two different kinds, or **sexes**, a male and a female. A tiny part of the male, called a **sperm**, joins up with a tiny part of the female, called an egg. This process is called **fertilization**. The new young creature that grows from the fertilized egg has some features of the male and some of the female. It is not exactly the same as either of its parents. This is called **sexual reproduction**.

▼ Human babies take many years to grow into adults. They must be cared for by their parents and other members of the family.

▼ Frogspawn floats in a pond. The female common frog lays about 2,000 eggs in just a few seconds. The male fertilizes them right after they have been laid.

Giving Birth

Sometimes, the fertilized egg grows inside the mother's body. Sometimes, it grows outside. Birds, fish, and many reptiles lay their eggs. The baby grows in the egg until it is ready to hatch. Fish and many reptiles can look after themselves as soon as they hatch. Baby birds have to be fed and kept warm in the nest.

The fertilized egg of many animals grows inside the mother's body. This includes the egg of a human being. The egg is kept safe and warm in the mother's body. When the baby is born, it cannot survive on its own. It needs milk from its mother's body. It has to be kept safe from danger while it grows and learns to take care of itself.

▼ A foal can stand and run almost as soon as it is born. But like human babies, it feeds on its mother's milk.

Female and Male

▼ For the first few years boys and girls have a similar body shape. As they grow into adults their bodies change, so that it is easy to see the differences between men and women.

The male and female kinds of every species are slightly different. They have different parts, or **organs**, which are made just for reproduction. The body of the human male produces sperm. The sperm fertilizes the female egg, and the egg eventually grows into a baby. The body of the human female is made so that a baby can grow inside her.

Men's Bodies

Men's bodies are larger and firmer than women's. Between their legs, men have an organ called a **penis**. The sperm leaves a man's body through his penis. Behind the penis is a bag of skin called the **scrotum**.

Inside the scrotum millions of sperms are made. They are made and stored in two **testes** inside the scrotum. The sperms travel from each testis to the penis along a tube called the **vas deferens**.

Sperms are too small to see with the naked eye. Millions and millions of sperms are made, but each female egg can only be fertilized by one sperm.

Women's Bodies

Women are usually slightly smaller than men. Their bodies have more fat for protection. Inside a woman's body are all the parts needed for a baby to grow. She has two small **ovaries** where the eggs are

6

made. The female egg is called an **ovum**. When there are more than one, they are known as ova. The human ovum is tiny. It is smaller than a pinhead.

When an ovum is ready, it travels out of the ovary down one of two **fallopian tubes**. The fallopian tubes lead to a pear-shaped organ called the **uterus**.

If an ovum is fertilized, it grows into a baby inside the uterus. When the baby is ready to be born, it comes into the world through an opening between the mother's legs. This opening is called the **vagina**.

Young babies cannot eat the same food as a child or adult. Their bodies cannot digest the kind of food we eat. Babies suck milk from their mothers' bodies. The milk is made in glands in the mothers' breasts. Babies do not usually need any other food to begin with. Mother's milk is the perfect food for several months.

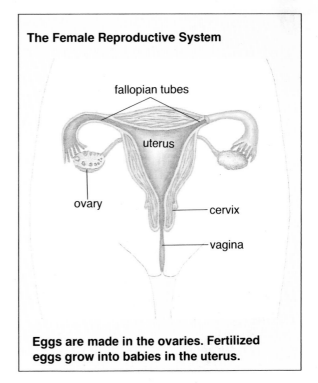

The Female Reproductive System

Eggs are made in the ovaries. Fertilized eggs grow into babies in the uterus.

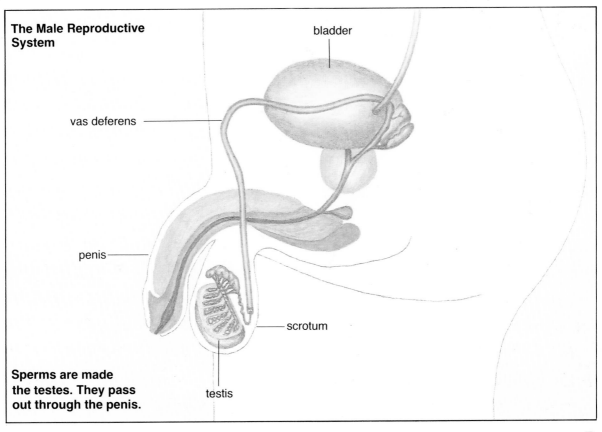

The Male Reproductive System

Sperms are made the testes. They pass out through the penis.

Body Changes

In the same way that a house is built of many bricks, our bodies are made of many tiny parts called **cells**. There are different kinds of cells in different parts of the body. A new human starts to grow when two special cells join. Those cells are a sperm cell from the father and an ovum from the mother.

The sperm and the ovum merge together. Then they start to divide, like an amoeba, but they do not separate. The cells divide and grow. They make up the millions of cells in the human body.

When humans are young, they cannot have babies or make sperms. It is only as they grow into adults that their bodies change. There are substances in the body which cause these changes. They are called

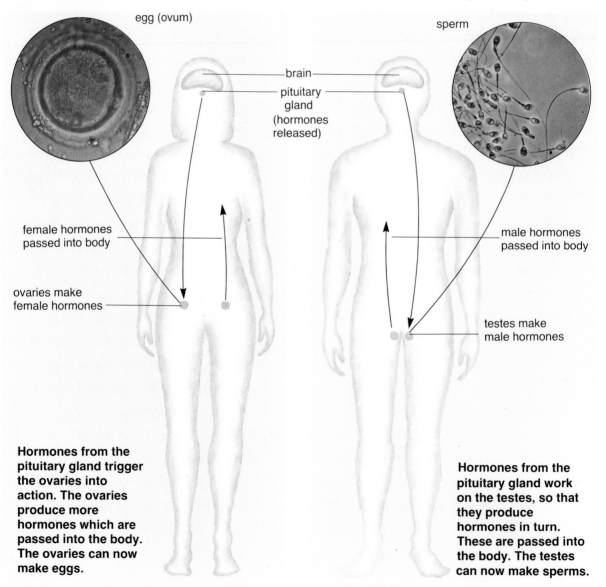

egg (ovum)

sperm

brain

pituitary gland (hormones released)

female hormones passed into body

ovaries make female hormones

male hormones passed into body

testes make male hormones

Hormones from the pituitary gland trigger the ovaries into action. The ovaries produce more hormones which are passed into the body. The ovaries can now make eggs.

Hormones from the pituitary gland work on the testes, so that they produce hormones in turn. These are passed into the body. The testes can now make sperms.

hormones. Hormones are made in **glands**. The hormones pour into the bloodstream and are carried around the body. They control many kinds of activity in our bodies. These include growth, sleep, and even how quickly we use up the food we eat.

There are also hormones that cause the male to make sperms and the female to produce ova. These hormones are called sex hormones.

▼ The hormone-producing glands cluster around the blood vessel. The hormones pass through the wall of the blood vessel into the bloodstream.

Hormones in Children

We all have sex hormones but in children the amount in their bodies is small. As children get older the levels of sex hormones increase. The sex hormones have different effects in males and females.

In boys, the hormones make the testes grow larger. They start to produce their own male sex hormones. As a result, sperms grow in the testes. In girls, the ovaries get larger and produce their own female sex hormones. Since a time before birth, many tiny eggs have been stored away in the ovaries. Now, they start to ripen. From time to time, a ripe ovum bursts out of one of the ovaries. If it meets up with a male sperm, a baby will begin to grow.

blood vessel

hormone-producing gland

Creating Life

A woman's body has to go through many changes to get it ready for a new baby to develop. Every twenty-eight days or so, hormones cause a ripe ovum to be swept out of one of the ovaries. The ovum moves gently along the fallopian tube until it reaches the uterus. If the ovum has not been fertilized by a sperm, it dies within two days.

The uterus has a special lining. This softens and fills with blood ready to receive the fertilized ovum. When the ovum dies, the lining is shed from the woman's body through the vagina. This shedding of the uterus lining is called **menstruation**. It happens every month and usually lasts four or five days. Then, the whole pattern starts again. Another tiny ovum journeys down the fallopian tube.

The Menstrual Cycle

ovum passes into fallopian tube

new uterus lining is formed

uterus lining breaks down

ovum dies if unfertilized

Every month, hormones make the ovaries release a ripe ovum. More hormones cause the uterus lining to become thicker and richly supplied with blood. If a fertilized ovum arrives in the uterus, it beds itself in the thick lining of the uterus. If the ovum has not been fertilized, the lining of the uterus peels away. It is shed, along with a small amount of blood, during menstruation.

Joining Together

To fertilize an ovum, the sperms have to get inside the female's body. The sperms leave the male's penis in a sticky white liquid called **semen**. The semen protects the sperms from damage. It also helps the sperms to move. When a male and female have **sexual intercourse** semen rushes out of the penis and into the vagina.

The semen contains hundreds of millions of sperms, but only one of them will join up with an ovum to fertilize it. The sperms have lashing tails that help them swim through the semen. They swim up into the uterus.

Only a couple of thousand sperms reach the openings into the fallopian tubes. The sperms swim into the tubes, searching for an ovum.

▲ This picture has been magnified many times. It shows human sperms trying to burrow into an egg, or ovum. Sperms produce a chemical which helps them pass through the outer layer of the egg and fertilize it.

When they find the ovum, they surround it and try to burrow into it through its outer wall.

When one sperm manages to get inside the ovum, the ovum is fertilized. The moment that the sperm is inside the ovum, the ovum changes and no other sperms can enter it.

Within a short time, the fertilized ovum divides into two cells, then four, then eight cells. This is the start of millions of cell divisions that will form a new human being.

In the Uterus

The fertilized ovum continues to move along the fallopian tube. It takes about a week to travel from the ovary to the uterus. When the ovum reaches the uterus, it burrows into the lining. The lining has thickened and is ready to receive it. The lining has a very good supply of blood. This blood provides food and oxygen for the growing group of cells.

Taking Shape

A woman with a baby growing inside her is said to be **pregnant**. She knows that she may be pregnant when she does not see the usual signs of menstruation. An ovum has been fertilized, so the lining of the uterus has not been shed.

By the time the mother has been pregnant for just seven weeks, the baby, or **fetus**, is less than a half inch long. However, many parts of the fetus are already recognizable as a human. The heart is already beating, and tiny arms and legs are starting to grow. By fourteen weeks the fetus is properly formed. It is still only about three inches long. It still has a lot of growing to do. The fetus could not yet survive on its own outside its mother's body.

There is still plenty of room for the fetus to move around. The mother may feel it moving at about sixteen to twenty weeks. At about sixteen weeks, the mother's stomach starts to get larger to make room for the growing fetus. At the end of pregnancy, her uterus has stretched to many times its normal size.

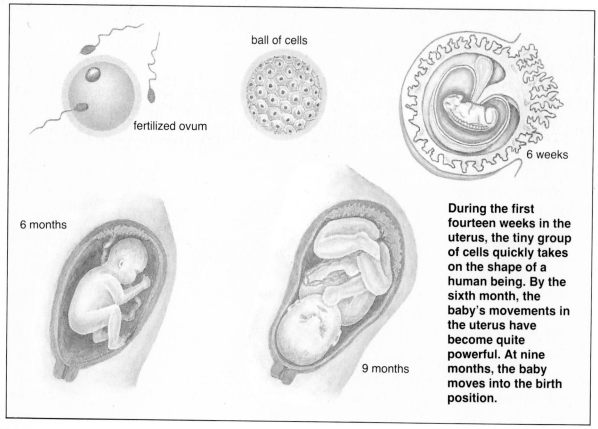

ball of cells

fertilized ovum

6 weeks

6 months

9 months

During the first fourteen weeks in the uterus, the tiny group of cells quickly takes on the shape of a human being. By the sixth month, the baby's movements in the uterus have become quite powerful. At nine months, the baby moves into the birth position.

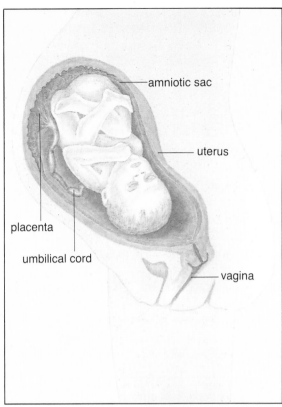

amniotic sac

uterus

placenta

umbilical cord

vagina

Life Support System

All the time the fetus is inside its mother, it is surrounded by a kind of bag. The bag is full of liquid called **amniotic fluid**. The fetus floats around inside the bag, or **amniotic sac**.

Even before it is born, the fetus needs food. The fetus gets the food from **nutrients**. These are tiny particles found in the mother's blood. A tube called the **umbilical cord** links the fetus to its mother. The umbilical cord is the fetus's lifeline. It leads to an organ called the **placenta**.

In the placenta, the fetus's blood comes very close to the mother's blood, although they do not actually mix. Nutrients and oxygen pass from the mother's blood to the fetus's. Wastes from the fetus go across to the placenta and into the mother's bloodstream to be washed away. Your belly button is the place where your umbilical cord once grew.

▲ The baby is curled up snugly in the uterus, protected by the fluid of the amniotic sac. The umbilical cord links the baby to the placenta, which acts as a life-support system.

► This baby has just been born. The umbilical cord is still attached to her stomach. Her skin is protected by a white greasy substance called vernix. Soon, she will open her eyes to see the world for the first time.

Giving Birth

After about forty weeks inside its mother's body, the new baby is ready to come out into the world. By this time, there is not much room for it to move about. Most babies have turned upside-down. They are usually born headfirst.

The **muscles** in our body make it possible for us to move. The uterus is made of very strong muscles. When a baby is ready to be born, hormones start movements in these muscles. These movements are called **contractions**. The muscles tighten for a minute or two and then relax.

First of all, this tightening of the muscle makes the opening of the uterus get larger. This opening is called the **cervix**. The cervix needs to be wide enough for the baby to squeeze through. This may take several hours and can be painful for the mother because these muscles may not have been used before. Before a baby is born, the amniotic sac surrounding the baby breaks, and the liquid inside pours out.

Into the World

When the cervix is fully open, or **dilated**, the baby's head can squeeze through into the vagina. More contractions push the baby out into the world. The baby takes its first breath on its own. It is time for the mother and father to see whether they have a boy or a girl. The mother can also take a rest after the hard work of giving birth.

Soon after the baby has been born, the umbilical cord is cut. This is painless for mother and baby. The placenta, which has now done all its work, is also pushed out through the vagina.

▼ **A baby is born. The muscles of the mother's uterus are very strong. They push the baby into the world headfirst.**

Birth

uterus contracting

umbilical cord

placenta

cervix

► Sometimes, babies are born too soon. Their bodies cannot keep warm so they are often put in an incubator. The incubator is a special box which keeps the babies warm and protects them from germs.

▼ The birth may take several hours. It is very hard work! At last, the baby is born and the mother can rest. These proud parents are delighted with their new baby.

Home or Hospital

For some women, home is the best place to have a baby. They feel secure in their own surroundings and with someone to help them. However, in many countries, most babies are born in a hospital. Both at home and in a hospital, there are specially trained nurses to help the mother and her baby during the birth. These nurses are called **midwives** or maternity nurses.

In a hospital, there is special equipment to keep checking on the baby or to help if the baby has trouble breathing. This has made childbirth safer for many mothers and their babies.

In many parts of the world, women have to give birth far away from well-equipped hospitals. Childbirth is still dangerous in these places. Mothers sometimes die from losing too much blood. Also, babies may be injured if the birth takes too long.

Some fathers want to be with their partners when their baby is born. Most parents look back on the births of their children as exciting and dramatic events. For the child, it is the most important birthday of his or her life!

Twins

Usually, a mother has only one baby at a time. However, some women give birth to two babies, or twins.

Looking Alike

Twins that look exactly alike are called **identical twins**. Right at the beginning of pregnancy, the fertilized ovum splits into two. Each half then grows into a separate complete baby. Each twin has its own amniotic sac, but they share just one placenta. While they are growing inside their mother, their bloodstreams actually mix in the placenta.

▼ Identical twins are always both either boys or girls. They grew from the same ovum and sperm so they are often very difficult to tell apart.

Because they grew from the same ovum and sperm, both babies are either boys or girls. They have the same hair and eye color. As they grow up they often become very close to each other. To anyone outside the family, it may be very hard to tell one from the other.

Looking Different

Normally, just one ovum is released from one of the ovaries at a time. Sometimes, more than one ovum is released. If two ova are fertilized by two sperms, then both the ova will grow into babies at the same time.

The mother will give birth to twins, but they will not be identical. Each grows from a different ovum and sperm. They have separate placentae. They may be different sexes and may have very different coloring. They are just like regular brothers and sisters except that they were born at the same time. These twins are called **fraternal twins**.

A single fertilized ovum splits into two. Each half grows into a separate baby. They share the same placenta and look exactly alike.

identical twins in uterus

single fertilized ovum divides in two

The ovary releases two ova at once. If both are fertilized, two babies grow in the uterus at once. They have separate placentae and may look quite different.

non-identical twins in uterus

two ova fertilized

More Than Two

Sometimes, two, three, or even more ova may be released. If all the ova are fertilized, then several babies will grow at once. The mother is said to have a **multiple birth**. Four babies are called quadruplets or quads, five babies are quintuplets, or quints. Six babies are called sextuplets, but they are very rare. Humans do not often give birth to more than two babies at once.

A woman may want to have a baby, but finds that she does not become pregnant. Doctors can give her drugs that help the ovaries to release their ova. The drugs may work too well. This is often the cause of a multiple birth.

▼ These children are quintuplets. All five were born at the same time. Because some are boys and some are girls and they do not look exactly alike, we know that several ova were fertilized at the same time.

The Body Program

While a mother is waiting for her baby to be born, she will probably wonder what it will look like. Will it be a boy or a girl? Will it have brown eyes or blue?

Just as a computer has a program to tell it what to do, so our bodies have a program to tell each part how to grow. This body program, or pattern, contains instructions for every detail about us from the color of our hair to the shape of our little toes. It takes the form of a chemical message which is passed on from parents to children at the moment when the sperm fertilizes the ovum. The code is stored away in tiny thread-like structures which are called **chromosomes**.

New Cells

Each cell in your body has forty-six chromosomes, which are arranged in pairs. However, the sperm and ovum have only twenty-three chromosomes each. At the moment of fertilization, the twenty-three chromosomes from the mother's cell pair up with the twenty-three chromosomes from the father's. This makes the full total of forty-six.

When the fertilized egg divides, a copy of the forty-six chromosomes is made for each new cell. Every one of the millions and millions of cells in your body will contain a copy of the original chromosomes. This makes up your body program.

▼ The ovum contains twenty-three chromosomes from the mother. The sperm has twenty-three chromosomes from the father in its head. This new baby has half her chromosomes from her mother and half from her father. She will look like both of her parents.

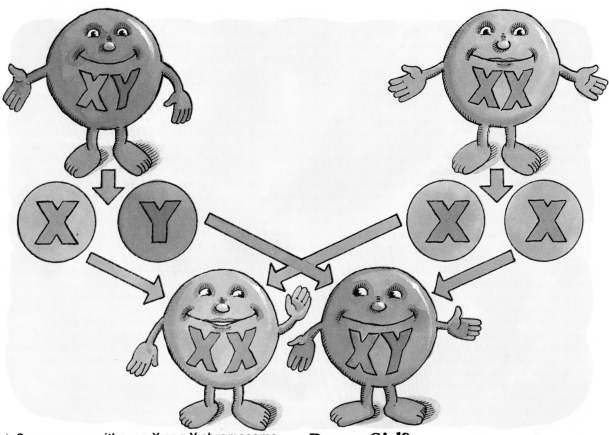

▲ Sperms carry either an X or a Y chromosome. If an X chromosome from the father joins with an X chromosome from the mother, the baby will be a girl. If a Y chromosome joins with the X from the mother, the baby will be a boy.

▼ These are greatly magnified chromosomes from one cell. They are grouped in twenty-three pairs. The last pair is not made up of a matching pair. They are an X and a Y chromosome. This shows that the cell comes from a boy.

Boy or Girl?

Your forty-six chromosomes are like steps in a knitting pattern. Each step contains the instructions for a different part of you. The ovum and sperm cells contain just one chromosome each which give the instructions for making a boy or a girl. These are the sex chromosomes.

The sex chromosome in the ovum is always called an X chromosome. The sex chromosome carried by the sperm can be either an X or a Y chromosome. If an X chromosome from the father joins the X chromosome from the mother, the developing baby will be a girl. If the sperm carries a Y chromosome, it will be a boy.

It is pure chance whether the fertilizing sperm carries an X or a Y chromosome. If doctors could separate out the X and Y carrying sperms, parents might be able to choose whether to have a boy or a girl. So far, doctors have had no success.

From Parents to Child

There are nearly five billion people in the world, yet every human being is unlike any other. This is because we each have our own set of chromosomes to make up our own body pattern. This body pattern is different from anyone else's.

Chromosomes are made of strings of separate blocks called **genes**. Genes are like packets of information or instructions. How tall we grow, whether we will be star football players or pianists depends largely on the genes with which we are born.

Family Likenesses

Your genes were passed on to you from your parents. Half came from your mother and half from your father. This is why members of families often look like each other. The genes that gave your grandmother curly hair may have been passed on to your mother, and then in turn to you.

The way genes are passed on from one generation to the next is called **heredity**. The study of genes and how they work is called **genetics**.

▼ Three generations line up for a family photograph. Can you see any family likeness?

Heredity or Surroundings?

Brothers and sisters may grow up to look very similar to each other, but be very different in character. However, they may look very different, but be alike in character. Usually, brothers and sisters share half of the same genes.

Some of the things people inherit in their genes cannot be changed. Other things are affected by what happens around them, or **environment**. For example, your genes might mean that you enjoy music. However, if you do not have the chance to learn the piano, you are unlikely to become a great pianist.

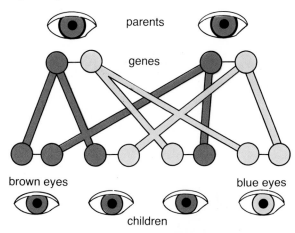

parents

genes

brown eyes

blue eyes

children

There are several types of skin and many eye colors. Your skin type and the color of your eyes are laid down in your genes and cannot be altered. Some genes are stronger than others. For example, the gene for brown eyes is stronger than the one for blue eyes. If both parents have blue eyes, their children will almost certainly have blue eyes, too. However, if both parents have brown eyes, there is still a small chance that they will have blue-eyed children. This happens if one of the grandparents or great-grandparents had blue eyes. If one parent has blue eyes, and one has brown, their children are more likely to have brown eyes.

Survival Kit

A newborn baby has not yet had time to learn about the world in which he finds himself. However, a new baby will suck milk without learning how to do it. He or she will also cry loudly when hungry, until food is provided. Both these kinds of behavior make sure that the baby gets the food he needs to survive and grow. They are examples of **instinct**. Instincts are passed on to us in our genes.

▲ What color are your eyes? Are they the same color as your parents' or your grandparents'? Eye color depends on genes passed on from one generation to the next.

▶ Babies cannot talk, but they can certainly yell! They do this to let us know that they need attention. They might be tired, hungry, or in pain.

Newborn Babies

The moment of birth is a time of great change for babies. For nine months they have been curled up in the warmth and safety of their mothers' bodies. A steady supply of food and oxygen has been piped in through the umbilical cord. Their mothers' bodies have done all the work of breathing and taking in food for them.

Within a few seconds of arriving in the world, they have to take their first gulp of air. Their lungs fill and start working on their own. Very soon after birth, their mothers' blood supply to the umbilical cord shuts down. Once the cord has been cut, the babies are on their own.

▼ Young babies get their food from milk. As they grow older, they need to have different foods. At first, food has to be smooth and easy to swallow because babies do not have teeth.

▲ A baby sleeps in his mother's arms. Babies become used to the rocking and swaying of the mother's body when they are in the uterus. A newborn baby sleeps much longer than an adult.

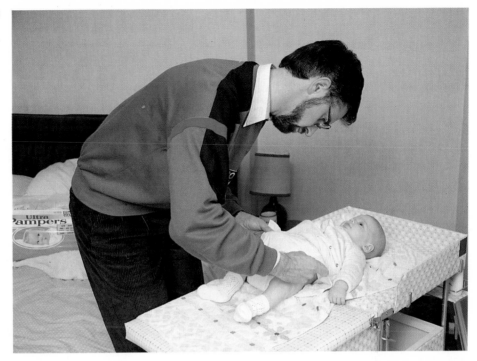

▶ Young babies stare at human faces. They soon learn to tell their parents' faces from others. From about six weeks old, babies can smile at their parents.

Programmed to Survive

At birth, babies do not know anything about the world in which they find themselves. They cannot move about or even feed themselves. However, they are not as helpless as they look. They can suck milk strongly. They can cry loudly when they are cold, hungry, or uncomfortable. In a very short time, they learn to recognize and respond to the people who are caring for them.

Food

Babies have to adjust to a new way of feeding as well as a new way of breathing. For the nine months before birth, food has been supplied in a ready-to-use form, straight from the mother's blood supply. After birth the best food for babies continues to come from their mothers as milk from their breasts.

Milk is made by hormones which work on glands in the mothers' breasts. The milk contains the right complex mix of nutrients that the baby needs. For the first few days, the early milk, or **colostrum**, is full of extra nutrients.

The baby nuzzles against the breast and fastens onto the tip of the breast, or nipple. The baby can then suck out the breast milk. The more the baby sucks, the more glands in the breast make milk to keep him or her satisfied.

Babies need to be fed very often in the first few weeks after the birth. It is a few months before their teeth begin to grow and babies learn to chew solid food.

Babies and Sickness

Our bodies have to learn how to fight off disease. Our blood supply learns to recognize **germs** that invade the body. To fight these germs, the blood makes **antibodies**. These antibodies stay in the blood and defend us against the germs the next time they strike.

The antibodies in the mother's blood protect the growing fetus in the uterus. The antibodies in her breast milk help to protect the young baby against disease.

Learning to Move

▼ Most babies go through a similar pattern of development. They have to gain control of the muscles in their backs before they can sit, crawl, or walk. Some babies never learn to crawl. They go straight from sitting on the floor to standing and walking.

During pregnancy, babies lie curled up in the uterus. At birth, they unfold and stretch out their legs and back for the first time. Their bony framework, or **skeleton**, is fully formed. At this stage, however, much of it is made of a tough tissue called **cartilage**. Cartilage is softer than bone, but over the next few years it will gradually harden.

An adult has 206 separate bones. A baby has about 350. In time, some of the baby's bones will grow together. For example, a baby's skull is made of separate plates. This allows the head to "give" a little as it is squeezed down through the mother's vagina at birth. During the first few years, the plates grow together. They form a rigid box which protects the brain.

Moving About

Like children and adults, every baby is different from every other. Some cry a lot. Some do not. Some begin to grow teeth at six months. Some do not start until they are a year old. However, as babies grow, one change usually follows after another in the same set order.

At birth, babies have little control over their muscles. They can move their arms and legs, and turn their heads. However, they cannot sit, roll over, or even lift up their heads. Over the next few weeks, babies gradually get control over the muscles in their necks. By about six weeks, a baby can hold its head up for just a second or two. A few days later, he or she can hold it up long enough to look around.

Gradually, the baby develops muscle control elsewhere in the body. When a baby is first sat on the floor, he or she will probably roll forward, back sagging. Not until six or seven months of age can most babies sit with a straight back. Then, one day, they will try to reach out for a toy. They will find themselves rolling forward onto their hands and knees. Soon they make their first crawling movements.

The more babies use their muscles, the stronger they get. Before they are a year old, many babies are trying to pull themselves up onto their feet. By instinct, they reach out for help from anyone who will help them. Even a piece of furniture will do.

▼ Many babies will practice walking for hours. They often fall over. They must learn to balance just as a circus clown learns to balance on a tightrope.

▼ In many countries, clinics are held so that doctors and other health advisors can check on babies. This helps to keep babies healthy.

Aware of the World

As soon as a baby comes into the world, he is surrounded by things to feel, hear, see, taste, and smell. All these things are called **stimuli**. From that first moment, a baby has to start separating and making sense of the flood of stimuli.

We do not know exactly how newborn babies sense the world. They cannot tell us what they see or hear. However, the way they behave gives us many clues.

The Senses

We know babies can feel. They like to be cuddled and held firmly. This will calm and soothe a fretful baby. We know they can hear clearly because they jump if startled by a sudden noise. They also respond to the sounds of voices by turning their heads to listen. They can do this from the first three or four days after they are born. If they are crying, they may be soothed by a recording of a heartbeat. This is the sound they have been listening to throughout the nine months of pregnancy.

We know that at first babies are **nearsighted**. This means that they only see clearly over a distance of nine to ten inches. Beyond this range, things look blurred. Babies will tend to look at a light patch across the room such as a bright window. They respond better to things held close to them, especially the human face. Babies seem to learn and recognize the faces of the people such as their parents who are taking care of them from very early on in their lives.

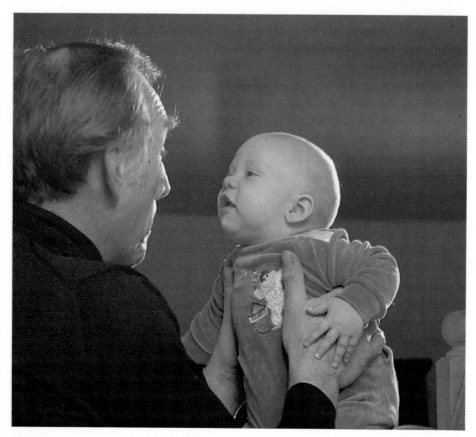

◄ This baby is studying his grandfather's face very closely. He is using his eyes and ears to try to make sense of what he is seeing and hearing.

▼ As children grow up, they may need check-ups to make sure they can hear properly. This child should turn in the direction of the rattle if her hearing is all right.

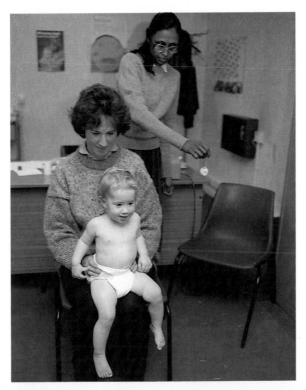

The flavor of food and drink is picked up by structures called **taste buds**. In adults, these taste buds are found mostly on the tongue, and there are some elsewhere in the mouth and in the throat. Babies have many more taste buds than adults. Also, their taste buds are found everywhere inside the mouth.

The First Year

Babies learn about the world around them by using all their senses. They pick up toys, look at them, touch them, and then bite and chew them. Bit by bit, they learn what is likely to be good to eat, or when something will be painful because it is prickly or too hot or too cold.

At the same time, their senses develop so that they can respond in more ways to different stimuli. They also begin to make sense of the babble of language that they have been hearing since birth.

▼ This child is concentrating on his toy. His senses are telling him about its color, shape, and whether it is hard or soft.

Speech

The ability to speak to each other is what makes human beings different from every other animal. By using language in the form of speech, reading, and writing, we can exchange complex ideas and store them for our children and their children in the years to come.

First Words

A small baby gets across his or her basic needs without needing speech. Most mothers can tell if their babies are tired, hungry, or in pain by the differences in the tone or strength of their cries.

In the first few months, as well as crying, babies make gentle cooing noises. As the baby gets older, the noises become more varied. Babies do not just copy sounds like talking parrots. Babies learn language by hearing it being used. They understand a great deal before they start to talk themselves.

Towards the end of the first year, many babies say their first words. These are likely to be labels for things that give them pleasure, for example people, animals, or favorite things. "Mummy," "dog" or "cookie" are good examples. In their second year they usually learn to add new words to those labels. Now they might say "more cookie" or "where teddy." In the second and third year, there is a great advance in language. Children begin to put together words to make sentences. By the age of five, they are using 1,200 to 2,000 words. Some adults know 25,000 words or more.

▼ Small babies make a stream of sounds. This gradually turns into single words. Simple speech is often helped along by pointing.

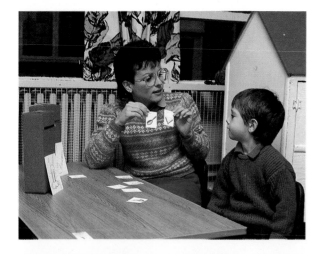

▼ Children who cannot hear properly often have trouble pronouncing difficult sounds. This speech therapist is teaching this child the difference in sound between the words "pan" and "fan."

Speech Problems

Some children have problems learning to speak. The most serious speech problems are caused by deafness. Babies born deaf cry normally. For the first few months, they make the same babbling noises as hearing babies. Soon the babbling dies down. It does not develop into speech because a deaf baby cannot hear the language around him. For deaf children, learning to communicate is a slow and difficult process. Trained teachers called speech therapists can help.

▼ Very deaf children often cannot speak clearly at all. They cannot hear what the words should sound like. They are taught sign language so they can "speak" using their hands. Each letter and some common words have special signs.

Using Your Brain

▼ Children have a built-in curiosity about the world around them. Games such as this help them to discover the difference between solids and liquids and to judge spaces and distances.

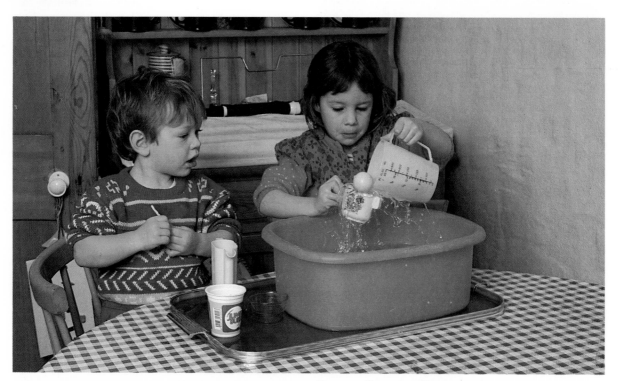

The brain is the body's control center and information storage area all rolled into one. It controls, directly or indirectly, everything that happens in our bodies.

At birth, the brain is large compared with other parts of a baby's body. If you look at a newborn baby, the head often seems too big for the tiny body and stick-like legs. The brain is already a quarter of the weight of an adult brain. A baby's body is only a twentieth of its adult weight. The brain grows fast. By the time the baby is one year old, the brain is half its adult weight. By the age of seven, the brain is almost fully grown. From then on, growth slows down. The brain will have reached its full size by the time we are about twenty years old.

Learning to Learn

From the moment of birth, babies build on the instincts with which they were born. They start to learn from the mass of stimuli coming in through all their senses.

The cells that receive these stimuli are called **nerves**. We have nerve endings all over our bodies. They pick up many details about shape, size, color, smell, taste, or pain. The information travels along the nerves to the brain where it is then stored.

The brain can also send out instructions along the nerves. These instructions control every movement we make, whether we are picking up a glass to drink from or playing a piece of music on the violin. This web of brain and nerve cells is called the **nervous system**.

At birth, many of the connections between brain and nerve cells have not fully grown. In the first weeks and months, whole new pathways are built in the brain. As the nervous system grows and matures, babies learn how to get control of the various parts of their bodies. Babies may first find out that they can move their own hands when they reach out for a rattle or toy. Later on, they learn how to open and close their fingers to grip the toy.

▼ The picture on the left was painted by a two-year-old. The picture on the right was the work of a four-year-old. As we grow older, we learn to observe and to record what we see, and to control our muscles.

Many babies go through a time when they seem to enjoy dropping things over the side of a crib or playpen. This is because they have finally gotten control over the nerves and muscles of the hand. This allows them to let go of things exactly when they want to. It can be very annoying for their parents!

A Busy Life

During the first five years, babies and young children learn faster than at any other time in their lives. During the first year, they learn about themselves, the things around them, their parents and family. In the second and third years, speech and language develop. This means that more and more complex ideas and experiences can be stored away in the memory.

Humans take about twenty years to become adults. This is longer than most other animals. Throughout the years of childhood, we learn new things all the time. As we get older, we go on learning. However, we never learn as quickly and easily as in the first few years of life.

▶ Young children like to have a story read to them before they go to bed. They learn to recognize pictures in the book. When they go to school, they learn to read for themselves.

Growing Bigger

We all started off as one tiny fertilized egg. How does that simple cell become a thinking, moving, fully-working human being? The answer is, by growing. Growth is a lot like a huge math problem. Cells divide in half, over and over again. The numbers get very large. In a full-grown adult there are millions and millions of cells.

However, the dividing cells are not all identical to each other. Different cells do different work. How do particular groups of cells know what they should become?

When the first cell division takes place, each new cell carries the complete instructions to make an entire new person. As further divisions take place, it seems that most of these instructions switch off.

They leave just the special information that will make the new cell grow into bone, muscle, or a big toenail.

Growing Bones

The most obvious way we grow is by getting taller. On our second birthday we are about half our final adult height. Most girls reach their final height at about fifteen. Boys reach theirs at about eighteen.

For us to grow taller, the long bones in our arms and legs have to get longer. Although bones look hard, they are living parts of our bodies. Bone cells get larger and divide just like any other cells.

Soon after birth, the ends of the long bones harden. In the middle of the bones, there is an area called a **growth plate**. At each end of the growth plate, the cells divide. This pushes the two ends of the bone further apart, making it longer. The growth plates gradually get smaller and disappear completely between the ages of twenty and twenty-four.

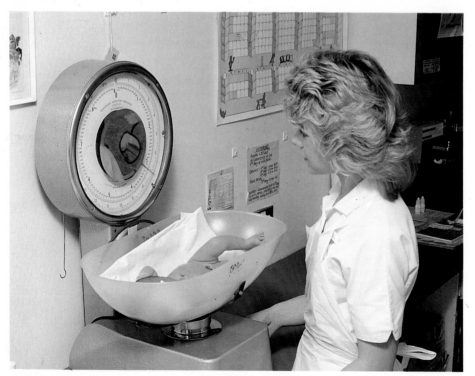

◄ In many countries, when babies are born, they are weighed. They are weighed again every few weeks to make sure that they keep on growing. Babies grow very quickly in the first year. They have usually doubled their weight before they are six months old.

▼ By the age of five years, many children have reached about two-thirds of their final height. Doctors keep a record of children's height to make sure that they are developing normally.

How Tall?

How tall we become depends on how fast we grow and for how long. This, in turn, depends on hormones. Growth hormone is made in the gland attached to the base of the brain, the **pituitary gland**. This growth hormone controls how fast we grow. Other hormones called **androgens** close the growth plates, and set our final adult heights.

Exactly how tall we finally become depends to some degree on the body pattern passed on in our genes. It also depends on the kind of food and care we get as children.

Not getting enough food, or eating food without the right balance of nutrients in it, can cause problems. This **malnutrition** means that children may not be as healthy nor grow as tall as they otherwise would.

▼ Even when we are fully grown, we will not all be the same height. These children are all the same age, but some are much taller than others. The ones who are short now may not be the shortest when they are adults.

Off to School

During the first five years, our body systems grow and develop at a great rate. At three years old, a child still has the chubby legs and arms, and the large head of a baby. By five, the babyish look has gone. Instead, there is a slim, leggy child.

At five years old, the brain is 75 percent of its adult weight. By six, it has reached 90 percent of its adult weight, and the nerve fibers are almost complete. For the first two or three years, children learn to make sense of what they hear, see, and feel. The people who are important to them are their parents, or whoever takes care of them, and any brothers and sisters. Two-year-olds like to be with other children but they often squabble with them. They have not yet learned how to share and co-operate with others.

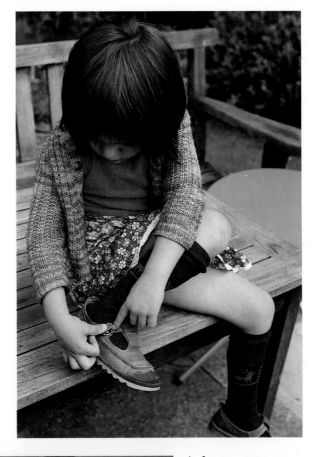

▲ As we grow, we are able to do very intricate tasks, like doing up shoe buckles.

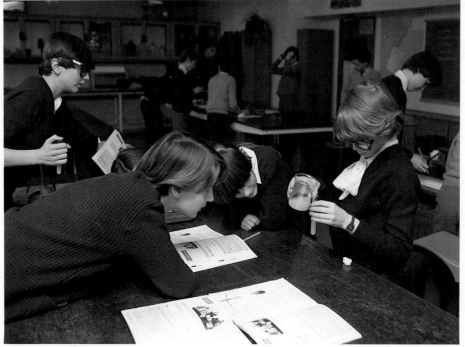

◄ At school, we do not simply memorize facts and figures by heart. We learn how to find out things for ourselves, and we learn very quickly. Only a few years before, these pupils would have been playing like the children on page 30. Now they can carry out scientific experiments.

Learning New Skills

During the school years, children continue to grow. They get stronger, and are able to move faster and more easily. They have already learned many basic skills, from how to walk and talk to how to feed themselves and put on their clothes. Children learn much of this simply by copying. Later, children can understand instructions. This helps them to learn a variety of new things, from tying their shoelaces to swimming or baking a batch of cookies. When a child reaches school age, children of the same age group, or **peers**, become important. Being accepted by our peers as part of the group is often more important even than fitting in at home.

Learning Through Play

"It's child's play," people say, to suggest that something is easy. However, child's play is more important than it looks. Playing with toys and with other children prepares children for the adult world.

Playing with a toy tea-set in a play house helps a five-year-old learn about size and shape. It is a way of copying skills from parents. Play also develops imagination with "let's-pretend" games. It also teaches children how to solve problems.

Later, through the rough-and-tumble of playground games, children learn how to respond to their peers. They find out how to deal with other people and to follow rules. Children also learn to tell the difference between right and wrong. It is all practice for the grown-up world when getting along with other people is no longer just a game.

▼ Dressing up as adults, and copying the things that adults do is an important part of growing up. These children are playing at "weddings." They have learned how to work together and to organize themselves, so they can each have a part to play.

Growing Up

Compared with many animals, humans are quite old before they can reproduce. During the last years of childhood, many changes take place inside our bodies. All these changes are preparing us to be able to have children of our own. This time of change between childhood and adulthood is called **puberty**.

Growing and Changing

Men and women have cells that come together to make a new baby grow. The biggest difference between the male and the female is that a new baby has to live and develop for nine months inside the female's body. Afterwards, the mother can still feed the baby with milk from her own body.

The changes needed to prepare both male and female bodies for all this are brought about by hormones. During childhood, the brain makes more and more of two special hormones. When these hormones have built up to a certain level, they cause other hormones to be released from the testes in boys and from the ovaries in girls. These hormones gradually spread all over the body.

In girls, the increase in hormone levels happens between about ten and twelve. It starts to bring about the body changes of puberty. The girl's breasts begin to develop. Hair begins to grow under her arms and between her legs. The most important sign of puberty comes when the first egg is released from the ovaries. This signals that the monthly cycle of menstruation has begun.

In boys, puberty is often a little later. Sperms begin to be made. The body gets more muscular and hair grows on his chest, under the arms, and between his legs.

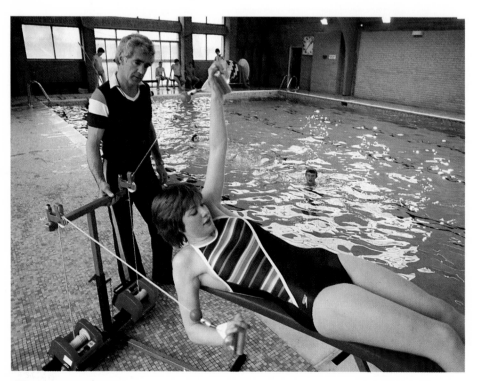

◀ As children reach puberty, their bodies change. They become stronger and better at many sports, particularly swimming. This girl is building up her muscles for swimming in competitions.

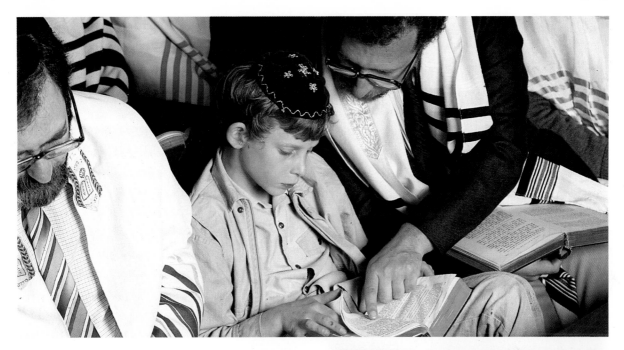

▲ This thirteen-year-old Jewish boy is preparing for his bar mitzvah. The ceremony will mark his passing from boyhood and his growing up. Similar ceremonies are held in many parts of the world.

Getting Together

For new life to be made, and for the human species to continue, couples must join together in the act of sexual intercourse. The changes that happen in puberty are all geared towards making reproduction possible. They also make the male and female more attractive to each other. This is the time when young people start getting interested in each other as boyfriends and girlfriends.

Some of the changes caused by hormones can be seen clearly. Other changes are not so obvious. During puberty, young adults still need their parents, but they must also make the first moves towards managing on their own. This is the time when they show this new **independence** in the clothes they wear, the hairstyles they choose, or in the interests they have.

▲ Teenagers like to develop in a way that is obviously different from their parents. These girls have formed their own rock group. They are probably not dressed as their mothers would be!

Adults and Families

The growth spurt of puberty comes to an end at about the age of eighteen. At this stage in their lives, teenagers are growing away from their parents. The skills learned throughout childhood now prove very useful. They are needed because becoming independent usually means getting a job and setting up a home.

Physically, a teenager of this age is ready to reproduce. That has been the purpose behind all the body's growth and development. Boys reach the peak of their reproductive lives between the ages of twenty and twenty-four. This means that they are most capable of reproducing, or **fertile**. Girls are most fertile a little later, at about twenty-four. Of course, many people have children earlier and later than this.

Having a Family

A human child needs years of care. It is usually the mother and the father who help and support him or her through this time.

Unlike most animals, human parents usually live together with their children. Two parents living together with their children is a common pattern of family life. They often live together in a larger group with other relatives. This is called an **extended family**. Sometimes, the parents and children live alone together in a **nuclear family**.

These are not the only ways of bringing up children. Sometimes parents separate and bring up children alone. They may even remarry and then the family becomes extended. Sometimes, a husband has several wives. Sometimes, a wife has several husbands. In some parts of the world, the children in the community are looked after as a group.

Whatever the number of parents, stepparents, or guardians, a good family group will provide care, love, and a stable environment for the children.

The End of Having Children

Men can go on making sperms and fertilizing ova until old age. Women, however, cannot always produce ova. Once again, the change is brought about by hormones. Between the ages of about forty and fifty, there is a drop in the level of the hormone **estrogen** in a woman's body. This slows down and eventually stops the release of ova from the ovaries. When a woman's menstrual periods stop completely, the woman will no longer be able to become pregnant.

▲ Much of our adult life is spent running the household and raising children.

▼ In some parts of the world, people do not live in small nuclear families. In this long-house in Borneo, the children of many different families are all brought up together.

Growing Old

People are living longer than they used to. Thirty years ago, the average age all over the world was only about forty-seven years. By the end of this century, the average age is expected to go up to sixty-four years. As we get older, cells all over the body stop working as well as they do when we are younger.

Signs of Old Age

The first signs of old age vary. When hair goes grey it is an obvious sign of aging. This starts happening to many people in their forties, though it can be much earlier. There are cells in the skin which make a substance called **melanin**. Melanin gives hair its color. When melanin is no longer made, the outer layer of the hair is colorless, so that it looks gray.

▲ Hair usually keeps on growing until the end of our lives. However, it often looses its color after the age of thirty. The cells that make the hair color stop working. The hair becomes gray and then white.

◄ Women generally live longer than men. These twins are well over 90 years old. Although they are very old, they still enjoy life.

Wrinkles are another clear sign of aging. As we get older, the fibers in the skin get more stretchy. This means that the skin becomes less firm and falls into wrinkles. This happens even more if skin is exposed to sunlight. Faces usually look more wrinkled than any other part of the body.

▲ Now that they no longer have their own children to care for, many elderly people enjoy the company of their grandchildren.

Inner Signs

From the moment the brain is fully grown, it starts to age. Every day, from the age of about twenty, we loose 10,000 or so brain cells. This is still only a tiny fraction of the total number we are left with in old age. However, sometimes as people get older, the brain does not work as well as it used to. Some elderly people often find it hard to remember things that happened recently, while they can remember events from distant childhood very clearly.

Blood vessels, muscles, and bone all suffer in the aging process. Blood vessels often get narrower and the heart pumps the blood less easily. Muscles get smaller. As they are used less, they get weaker. Bone, too, is lost. As we get less active, our bones get lighter and more brittle. They are more likely to break under sudden pressure.

Getting old may sound a little gloomy. Yet, many elderly people feel younger than they look. Many eighty-year-olds look far younger than they actually are. Staying active by exercising keeps muscles and bones strong.

When People Die

▼ At this Christian funeral in Switzerland, the body is placed inside a wooden coffin. Members of the dead man's family carry flowers in his memory. The coffin will be buried in the ground.

There are things we can do to slow down the aging process. Exercise and the right kind of food help to avoid many of the diseases of the elderly. So far, however, no one has found a way of stopping the slow weakening of the body's organs. Eventually, everyone dies.

What Is Death?

As we get older, the heart, lungs, kidney, and liver work less and less well. To stay alive and healthy, our bodies rely on the heart to pump blood through a network of blood vessels. Blood carries the nutrients and oxygen we need to every cell in the body. In old age, the heart may not keep up with the demand for food and oxygen. It slows down and stops. When the heart stops beating, blood stops flowing. Cells all over the body are starved of food and oxygen. Different cells can last for a longer or shorter time. Brain cells can only survive for a matter of seconds without a blood supply.

A Time for Sadness

Most people want to live as long as they can. It is part of the natural drive to survive that is built into our genes. Yet, it seems that we are programmed to die when we get old, just as we are programmed to survive as newborn babies. This programming allows for change and variety.

The death of a friend or a family member is usually a time of great sadness. Knowing that the person is gone forever is often very hard to accept.

▲ When a body is burned, it is called cremation. At this funeral in Bali, Indonesia, the body is cremated with an elaborate ceremony.

In Memory

People all over the world have different ways of marking death. The body of the dead person is usually burned or buried in a ceremony called a **funeral**. In some countries, this is a time of sadness or **mourning**. In others, it is a time to celebrate life and the living. The funeral gives family and friends a chance both to remember the dead person and to say goodbye. Ceremonies like these help friends and family to accept death.

▲ These girls in the Philippines light candles at this service in memory of the dead.

43

What Will the Future Bring?

People have lived on the earth for about five million years. We started off as simple ape-like creatures. We learned to use tools. We learned the advantages of living in groups to make the best of food supplies.

As generation followed generation, genes mixed with genes. Our minds and bodies changed little by little. Gradually, we grew less ape-like and taller. Our brains grew bigger. A clever hunter had a better chance of surviving when times were hard and food was in short supply. It follows that his genes had more chance of being passed on to the next generation, and with his genes his hunting skills. This slow process of change happening generation by generation is called **evolution**.

The Peak of Achievement?

Will our bodies and minds continue to change and evolve? Perhaps, we have already reached the height of our strength and achievement. Today, we live in a world full of machines that are here to help us. Most of us no longer use our bodies to escape from animals or to hunt for food. If we need to travel faster or see further, we can use a car or a telescope. If we have trouble breathing or hearing machines can help us with these problems, too.

Test-Tube Babies

Sometimes, people find it difficult to have babies. In the last ten years, it has become easier for men and women who have these problems to have babies. Sperms and ova can now be collected and deep-frozen. Later on, the ovum can be fertilized and put back into the mother's uterus where it grows like any other baby. The mother no longer needs to be the person who makes the ovum. People can now offer their own sperms and ova to men and women who would not otherwise be able to have babies.

Scientists are now working on ways of separating X and Y-carrying sperms. This could mean that, in the future, we may well be able to choose to have either boys or girls. We may also be able to choose exactly when we would like to have them.

Modern Medicine

The first people did not have doctors or medicines. If they were hurt or became sick, they had to rely chiefly on the body's own defense system to heal itself. It was the weakest members of the group who died in an attack or from disease. Today, we have strong drugs to overcome many diseases. More of us than ever live to a ripe old age. Even if we are not 100 percent healthy, we can expect to survive in order to pass on our genes to the next generation. It is likely that a broader and broader mix of genes will be passed on to give shape to future generations of humans.

▼ In the future, people may be able to live in space. By that time, we may have mixed our genes so widely that people will look more alike. Also, we may know how to slow down the aging process.

Glossary

amniotic fluid: a watery liquid which surrounds an unborn baby. The fluid protects the baby.

amniotic sac: the bag-shaped tissue which surrounds a baby while it grows inside the mother.

androgen: a substance that helps bring about some of the changes in our bodies as we grow up. It also helps control how tall we grow.

antibody: a substance made by your body which protects the body against sickness.

cartilage: a tough, rubbery material found in various parts of the body. Some cartilage hardens into bone as we grow up.

cell: a very small part or unit of a living animal or plant. Most living things are made up of millions of cells.

cervix: the narrow opening into the part of the body where an unborn baby grows. The cervix gets much larger when the baby is to be born.

chromosome: a tiny thread-like structure found in every one of your cells. Chromosomes are found in pairs and carry the instructions for how every part of the body will grow.

colostrum: milk that is made just after a baby is born. It is very rich in important foods and helps protect the new baby from sickness.

contraction: getting smaller or drawing together. When a baby is ready to be born, the mother's uterus muscles draw together to push the baby out of her body.

dilate: to become larger or wider.

environment: the combination of people, places and things around us.

estrogen: a substance in the body which makes the female become able to have babies.

evolution: the way living things have reached their present form by slow and gradual change. This has happened over thousands of generations.

extended family: any family group which includes more than parents and children.

fallopian tubes: the tubes inside a woman's body that lead from where the eggs are stored to the uterus where an egg can grow into a baby. Eggs travel along the fallopian tubes to the uterus.

fertile: being able to make young.

fertilization: the moment male and female cells join up and start to grow into a baby.

fetus: the young of an animal in the uterus or in the egg.

fraternal twins: two babies who have grown from separate eggs in the same mother at the same time.

funeral: the ceremony that takes place when a dead body is burned or buried.

gene: the tiny parts in each living cell which makes up the pattern for how every part of the body will grow.

genetics: the study of how body patterns made by genes are passed on from one generation to the next.

germ: a tiny living thing which causes disease. Germs can be seen only with a very strong microscope.

gland: a part of the body which makes a substance for the body to use. Different glands make different substances.

growth plate: a part of the long bones where growth takes place. They gradually get smaller and disappear completely when the bones are fully grown.

heredity: the way certain features of the parents are passed on to the following generations.

hormone: a substance made in the body to trigger changes like growth. Hormones are carried around the body in the bloodstream.

identical: exactly the same.

identical twins: two babies who have grown from the same fertilized egg. The babies have the same body pattern and look exactly alike.

independence: being able to survive without depending on others.

instinct: behavior which we carry out without thinking or learning about it.

malnutrition: sickness caused by having too little food or by eating the wrong sort of food over a period of time.

melanin: a layer of dark coloring which is found in skin and hair.

menstruation: when the thick lining of the uterus leaves a woman's body, together with a small amount of blood.

midwife: someone who is trained to look after a mother while she is pregnant and at birth of the baby.

mourning: feeling sad when someone has died.

multiple birth: when a woman gives birth to more than one baby at a time.

muscle: a type of material in the body which tightens and relaxes to produce movement.

nearsighted: only being able to see clearly for a short distance.

nerve: one of a network of tiny fibers which pass messages from all parts of the body and brain.

nervous system: the interconnected network of nerves, brain, and spinal cord.

nuclear family: a family group made up of just the parents and children.

nutrient: the part of any food which can be used by the body for health and growth.

organ: a part of the body which has a particular job such as the brain or stomach.

ovary: one of the small structures in the female body where eggs are stored.

ovum: a tiny part in the female body which can be fertilized and grow into a new member of the species.

peer: a person in your age group who is similar to you.

penis: the part of the male body which lets out waste water and is used to fertilize the female egg.

pituitary gland: a small part of the body at the base of the brain. It makes several substances which help control functions in the body such as the rate of growth.

placenta: the structure that grows inside the mother's body to pass on food and oxygen to the unborn baby from the mother.

pregnant: when a female has a baby growing inside her. Different animals are pregnant for different lengths of time.

puberty: the time between about twelve years and eighteen years when the human body grows and develops from a child into an adult.

reproduction: the way plants and animals make new versions of themselves.

scrotum: the part of the male body that contains the cells which fertilize a female egg.

semen: a liquid made in the male body to carry the tiny cells which fertilize a female egg.

sex: one of either of two groups, the male or female, of any species.

sexual intercourse: when a male and female come together in the act which may make a baby.

sexual reproduction: a way of making a new plant or animal by joining some parts of the male and female of the same plant or animal.

skeleton: the framework of bones which supports the body of some animals.

species: a group of animals or plants which look alike and can breed with one another.

sperm: the tiny part of a male which joins with the female egg to make a baby. They are one of the smallest cells in the body.

stimuli: things that trigger action or have an effect on whatever they fall upon.

taste bud: a tiny part of the tongue which picks up different tastes. The tastes are sweet, sour, bitter, and salt.

testis: one of two parts of a male body which makes the cells used to reproduce young.

umbilical cord: the tube that joins the unborn baby to the mother. It carries food and oxygen from the mother's bloodstream to the baby's.

uterus: the part of a woman's body where an unborn baby grows. It is also called the womb.

vagina: the part of a woman's body through which a baby passes when it is being born.

vasa deferentia: one of the two tubes leading from the testes in the male body to the outside.

Index